PIANO / VOCAL / GUITAR

CONTEMPORARY CHRISTIAN

ISBN 978-1-4234-3869-4

CORPORATION

7777 W. BLUEMOUND RD. P.O. BOX 13819 MILWAUKEE, WI 53213

Visit Hal Leonard Online at
www.halleonard.com

CONTENTS

4   All About Love
     Steven Curtis Chapman

27   All I Need
     Bethany Dillon

13   All to You
     Lincoln Brewster

20   Angels
     Amy Grant

34   Atmosphere
     tobyMac

42   Be Near
     Shane & Shane

54   Breathe
     Jeremy Camp

51   The Coloring Song
     Petra

60   Come On Back to Me
     Third Day

68   The Concert of the Age
     Phillips, Craig & Dean

76   Deeper
     Delirious?

88   Dying to Reach You
     Point of Grace

83   Entertaining Angels
     Newsboys

96   Every Season
     Nichole Nordeman

102 Faithful to Me
     Kathy Troccoli

106 Filled with Your Glory
     Starfield

120 Free
     Steven Curtis Chapman

128 Go West Young Man
     Michael W. Smith

113 Gravity
     Shawn McDonald

134 Hallelujah
     Bethany Dillon

141 He Will Carry You
     Scott Wesley Brown

146 He'll Do Whatever It Takes
     Phillips, Craig & Dean

151 I Believe
     ZOEgirl

158 I Wanna Sing
     Scott Krippayne

174 I'll Be Believing
     Point of Grace

178 In a Little While
     Amy Grant

184 In the Light
     dc Talk

165 King
     Audio Adrenaline

190 Living Hallelujah
     Sarah Kelly

198 Look What You've Done
     Tree63

214 Love Heals Your Heart
     Third Day

220 Love One Another
     Michael W. Smith

226 Maker of All Things
Tree63

207 Oceans from the Rain
Seventh Day Slumber

234 Oh, I Want to Know You More
Steve Green

238 Pray
Darlene Zschech

244 Ready for You
Kutless

250 The Robe
Wes King

264 Song of Love
Rebecca St. James

270 Spirit Thing
Newsboys

276 These Hands
Jeff Deyo

255 This Is Your Life
Switchfoot

282 The Way I Was Made
Chris Tomlin

289 Welcome Home (You)
Brian Littrell

296 What If His People Prayed
Casting Crowns

304 What Matters Most
Cheri Keaggy

311 When You Spoke My Name
MercyMe

316 Where There Is Faith
4Him

331 Whole Again
Jennifer Knapp

324 Wisdom
Twila Paris

344 Wonder Why
Avalon

338 You're the Voice
Rebecca St. James

ALL ABOUT LOVE

Words and Music by
STEVEN CURTIS CHAPMAN

We've got

ALL TO YOU

Words and Music by LINCOLN BREWSTER
and REID McNULTY

You called me, Lord, ___ You know my name. ___
You are ___ the Lord ___ of all ___ I am. ___

I'm stand-ing now, ___ I'm not ___ a-shamed, ___
And I'll nev-er be ___ the same a-gain, ___

I'm giv-ing it all. _____

(Guitar solo)

ANGELS

Words and Music by AMY GRANT,
GARY CHAPMAN, MICHAEL W. SMITH
and BROWN BANNISTER

"Take this man to pris - on," the man ___ heard Her - od say, ___ and
on - ly knows the times ___ my life was threat - ened just to - day. ___ A

chains that bound the man of God just o-pened up and fell, and
en-e-my is clos-ing in, I know some-times they fight to

run-ning to his peo-ple be-fore the break of day, there was
keep my feet from fall-ing. I'll nev-er turn a-way. If you're

on-ly one thing on his mind, on-ly one thing to say:
ask-ing what's pro-tect-ing me, then you're gon-na hear me say: Got His

An-gels watch-ing o-ver me, ev-'ry move I make.
an-gels

D.S. al Coda

Got His

CODA

An - gels watch - ing o - ver me, an - gels watch - ing o - ver me,

ALL I NEED

Words and Music by BETHANY DILLON,
ED CASH and DAVE BARNES

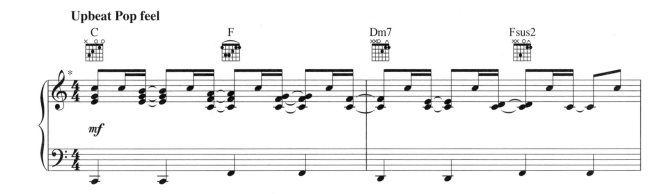

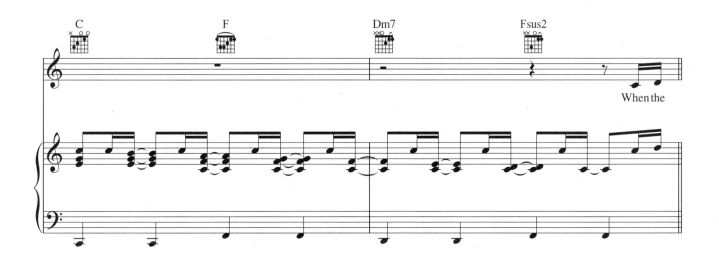

When the

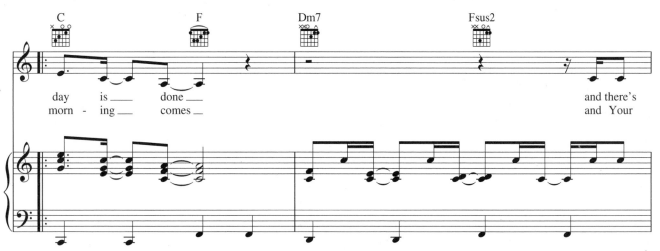

day is ___ done ___   and there's
morn - ing ___ comes ___   and Your

Recorded a half step lower.

You fill me _____ when _ I'm emp -

- ty. There is noth - ing else; ___ You're _ all I _____ need. _

When the

ATMOSPHERE

Words and Music by TOBY McKEEHAN,
RANDY CRAWFORD and JEFF SAVAGE

I know you keep a jour-nal and ev-'ry page is rip-pled from the
know you're all a-lone in a crowd full of friends; I can

tears that you cry. Ain't no mean-in' to your scrib-ble, 'cause words can't de-scribe what you been feel-in' in-side. It's like
see it in your eyes that you're fad-in' a-gain. Check-in' out, mov-in' in-to your hole where the

thou-sand foot walls and they're still on the rise. But look up to a beau-ti-ful sound and see
light can't touch an-y part of your soul. But hold up, and let the riv-er rush in.

mov - in' in - to your at - mos - phere. _____ (Said I'll be there al - ways, for - ev - er.)

there. _____

Repeat and Fade

Optional Ending

BE NEAR

Words and Music by
SHANE BARNARD

You are ___ all, ___

to us ____ our _____ good, _____

my ____ good.

THE COLORING SONG

Words and Music by
DAVE EDEN

Moderately slow, in 2

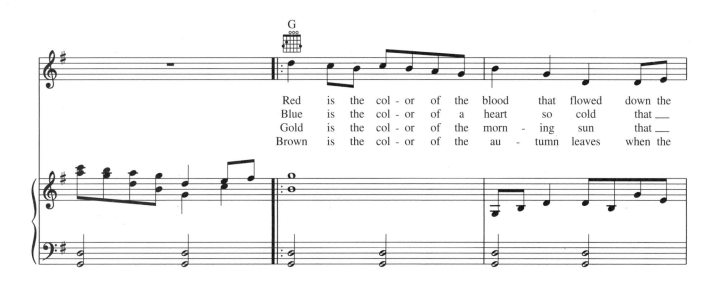

Red is the col-or of the blood that flowed down the
Blue is the col-or of a heart so cold that ___
Gold is the col-or of the morn-ing sun that ___
Brown is the col-or of the au-tumn leaves when the

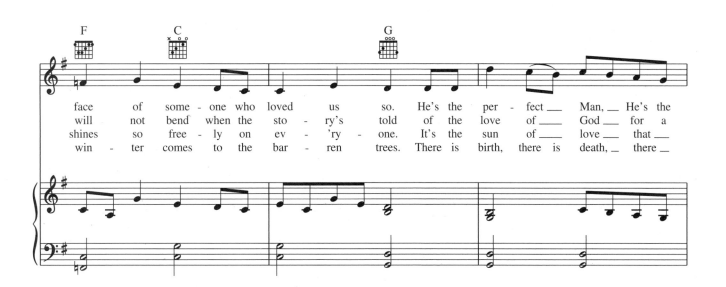

face of some-one who loved us so. He's the per-fect ___ Man, ___ He's the
will not bend when the sto-ry's told of the love of ___ God ___ for a
shines so free-ly on ev-'ry-one. It's the sun of ___ love ___ that ___
win-ter comes to the bar-ren trees. There is birth, there is death, ___ there ___

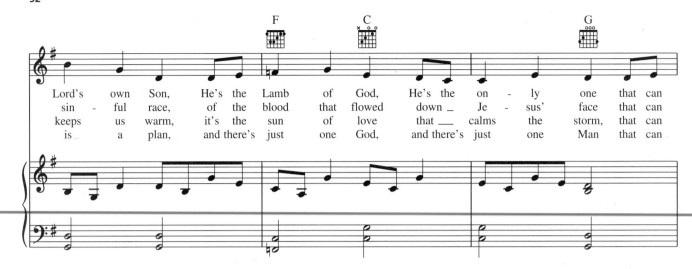

Lord's own Son, He's the Lamb of God, He's the on - ly one that can
sin - ful race, of the blood that flowed down _ Je - sus' face that can
keeps us warm, it's the sun of love that _ calms the storm, that can
is a plan, and there's just one God, and there's just one Man that can

give us life, that can make us grow, that can make the love be -
give us life, that can make us grow, that can keep our hearts from _
give us life, that can make us grow, that can turn our morn - ings _
give us life, that can make us grow, that can make our sins as ____

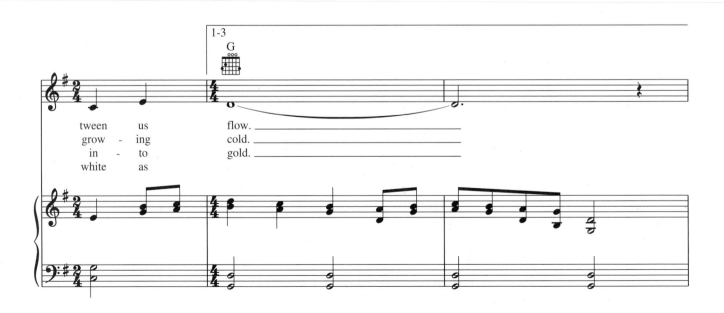

tween us flow. _____
grow - ing cold. _____
in - to gold. _____
white as

BREATHE

Words and Music by JEREMY CAMP
and ADAM WATTS

COME ON BACK TO ME

Words by MAC POWELL
Music by TAI ANDERSON, BRAD AVERY,
DAVID CARR, MARK LEE and MAC POWELL

Well, you've been hid - ing now for so ___ long

THE CONCERT OF THE AGE

Words and Music by GEOFF THURMAN
and JEOFFREY BENWARD

DEEPER

Words and Music by MARTIN SMITH
and STUART GARRARD

Moderate Rock Shuffle

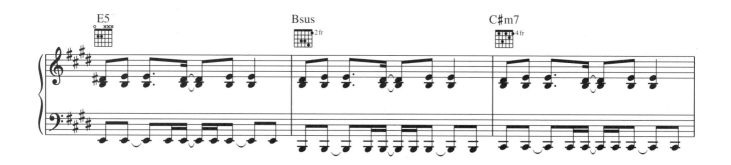

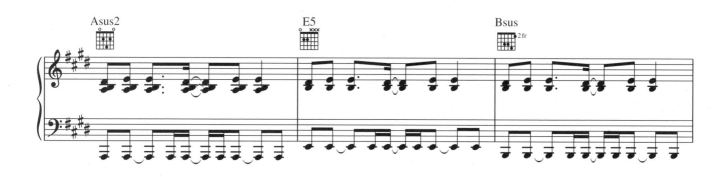

I want to go

ENTERTAINING ANGELS

Words and Music by PETER FURLER,
PHIL URRY and JODY DAVIS

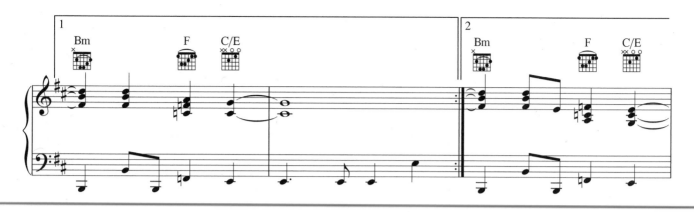

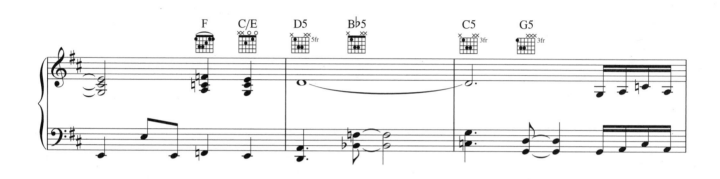

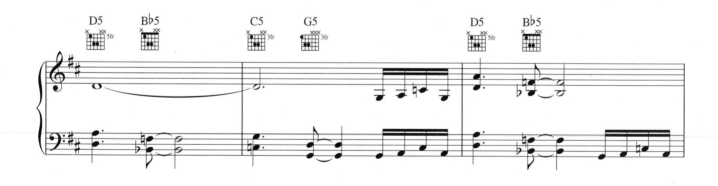

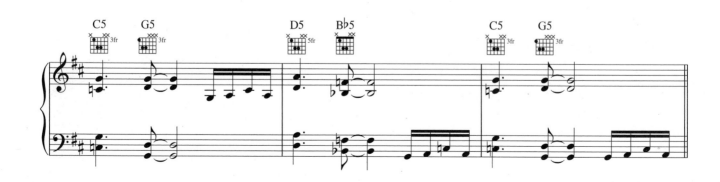

87

DYING TO REACH YOU

Words and Music by MICHAEL PURYEAR
and GEOFFREY THURMAN

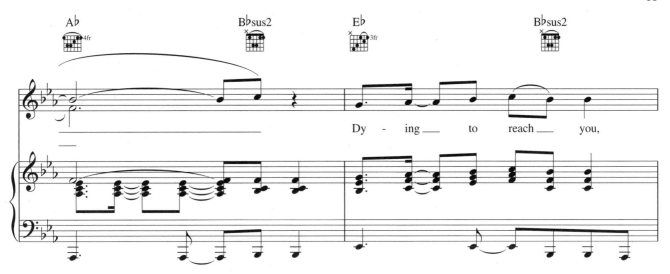

Dy - ing___ to reach___ you,

to reach you.___ Dy - ing___ to reach___ you.___

EVERY SEASON

Words and Music by
NICHOLE NORDEMAN

FAITHFUL TO ME

Words and Music by KATHY TROCCOLI
and SCOTT BRASHER

FILLED WITH YOUR GLORY

Words and Music by TIM NEUFELD
and JON NEUFELD

Yeah.

GRAVITY

Words and Music by SHAWN McDONALD
and CHRIS STEVENS

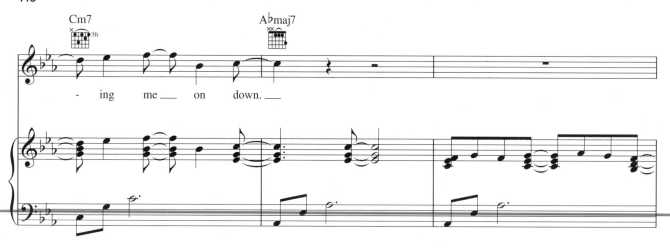

-ing me __ on down. __

I don't wan-na fall __ a - way __ from You. __

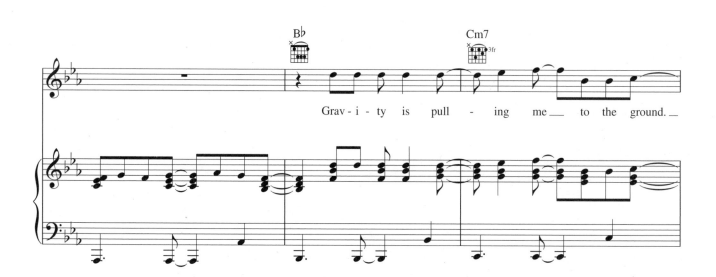

Grav-i -ty is pull - ing me __ to the ground. __

FREE

Words and Music by
STEVEN CURTIS CHAPMAN

GO WEST YOUNG MAN

Words by WAYNE KIRKPATRICK
Music by MICHAEL W. SMITH

I'm blaz - ing __ a trail __ that leads __ to vice, __ so
Why must I wan - der like __ a cloud, __

eas - i - ly __ en - ticed __ by dark - er __ means. __
fol - low - ing __ the crowd? __ Well, I don't __ know. __

When out of __ the wil - der - ness __ of choice __
But I'm ask - ing for __ the will __ to fight, __

Recorded a half step higher.

Copyright © 1990 by Universal Music - Careers and Sony/ATV Music Publishing LLC
All Rights on behalf of Sony/ATV Music Publishing LLC Administered by Sony/ATV Music Publishing LLC, 8 Music Square West, Nashville, TN 37203
International Copyright Secured All Rights Reserved

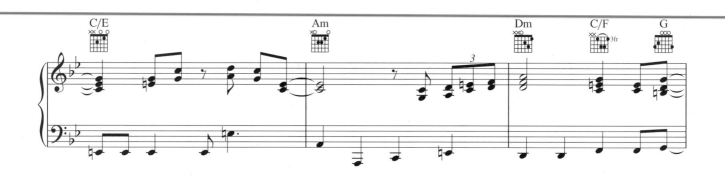

The mind _ is _ weak, the heart _ is frail _

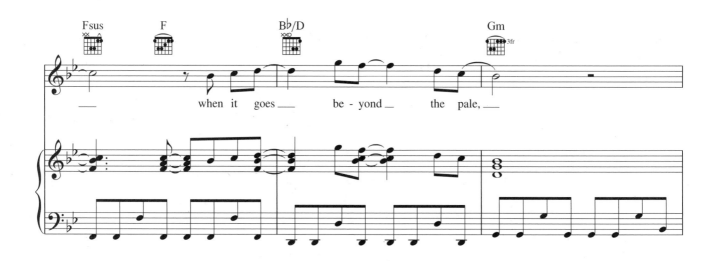

_ when it goes ___ be - yond ___ the pale, ___

HALLELUJAH

Words and Music by BETHANY DILLON
and ED CASH

Who can hold the stars ___ and my wea - ry heart? ___
___ Who can see ev - 'ry - thing? I've fall - en so ___ hard, ___
___ some - times I feel so far, but not be - yond ___ Your ___

HE WILL CARRY YOU

Words and Music by
SCOTT WESLEY BROWN

HE'LL DO WHATEVER IT TAKES

Words and Music by
DAN DEAN

You don't know just how far away from home I've been
I've heard His love is patient, that He always hears a prayer and that His

she said as she looked into my eyes.
love will fol - low you despite the miles.

My best

I BELIEVE

Words and Music by
ALISA GIRARD

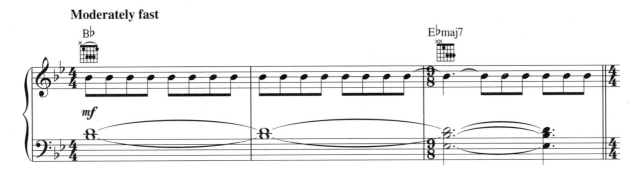

Ooh.

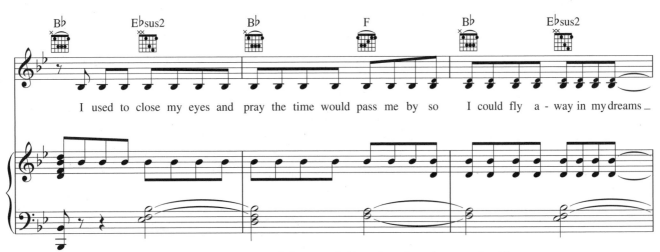

I used to close my eyes and pray the time would pass me by so I could fly a - way in my dreams

Original key: B major. This edition has been transposed down one-half step in order to be more playable.

He comes to sweet - ly _____ say, _____ "It's

all gon - na be o - kay." _____ Now I'll shout

_____ it from _ the moun - tain.

Now I'll shout _____ it from _ the moun - tain.

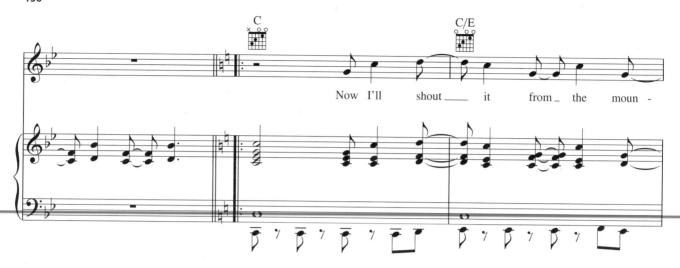

Now I'll shout ___ it from the moun -

- tain, that I'm not the same ___ that I ___ used to ___ be.

I be - lieve ___ in God, ___ be - lieve ___ in God. (I be - lieve ___ in God.) ___

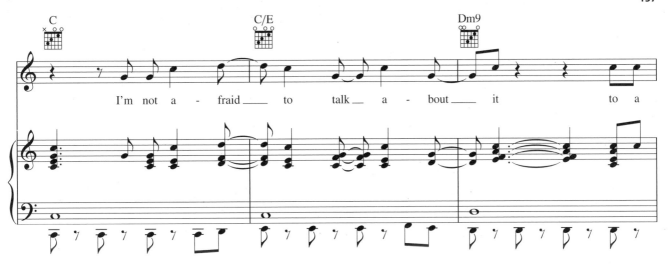

I'm not a-fraid____ to talk____ a-bout____ it to a

world that slow - ly slips____ a - way,____ that I be-lieve____ in God,____

(I be - lieve____ in God.)____

____ be - lieve____ in God.____

I WANNA SING

Words and Music by SCOTT KRIPPAYNE,
KYLE MATTHEWS and KENT HOOPER

KING

Words and Music by MARK STUART,
WILL McGINNISS, BOB HERDMAN,
TYLER BURKUM and BEN CISSELL

I'LL BE BELIEVING

Words and Music by GEOFFREY P. THURMAN
and BECKY THURMAN

IN A LITTLE WHILE

Words and Music by BROWN BANNISTER,
AMY GRANT, SHANE KEISTER
and GARY CHAPMAN

With emotion

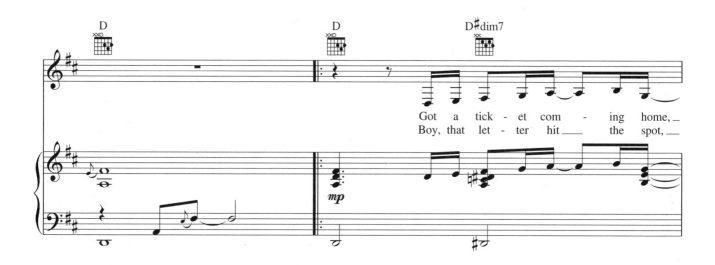

Got a tick - et com — ing home, _

Boy, that let - ter hit __ the spot, _

__ wish the of - fi - cer __ had known __ what a day to - day __ has been. __

made me think of all __ I've got ____ and __ all that waits for me. _

IN THE LIGHT

Words and Music by
CHARLIE PEACOCK

LIVING HALLELUJAH

Words and Music by
SARAH KELLY

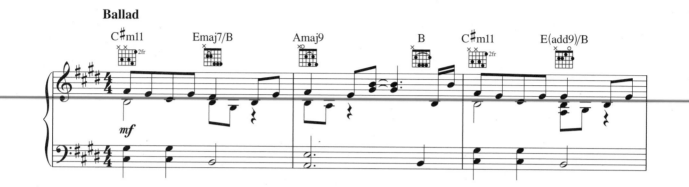

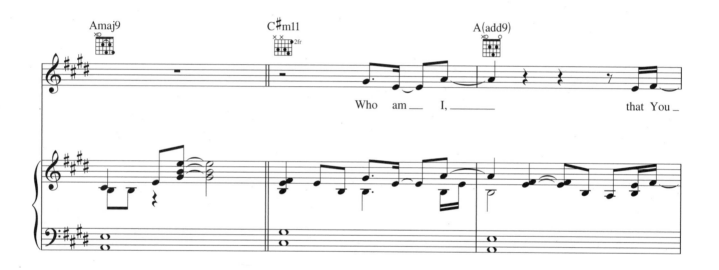

Who am I, ___ that You ___

___ came to Earth for me ___ to die on ___ a ___ tree? ___

LOOK WHAT YOU'VE DONE

Words and Music by
JOHN ELLIS

OCEANS FROM THE RAIN

Words and Music by
JOSEPH ROJAS

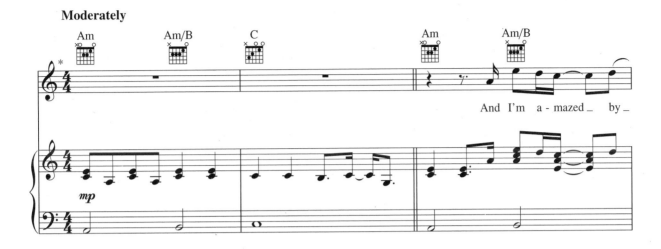

And I'm a-mazed __ by __

__ You, 'cause You're nev-er far __ a-way. __

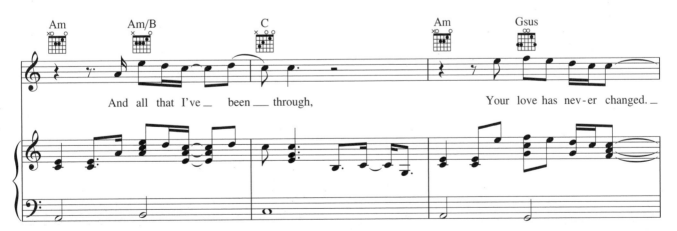

And all that I've __ been __ through, Your love has nev-er changed. __

Recorded a half step lower.

LOVE HEALS YOUR HEART

Words by BRAD AVERY
Music by MAC POWELL, DAVID CARR,
TAI ANDERSON, BRAD AVERY and MARK LEE

Love _ heals _ your _ heart. _

When you think __ your life __ is shat-tered and there's no _

Love, it   heals _ your heart, _   now. _____   Oh. _____

Repeat ad lib. and Fade

Optional Ending

LOVE ONE ANOTHER

Words and Music by MICHAEL W. SMITH
and WAYNE KIRKPATRICK

MAKER OF ALL THINGS

Words and Music by
TIM HUGHES

Earth joins ___ with heav - en ___ de - clar - ing ___ Your

OH, I WANT TO KNOW YOU MORE

Words and Music by
STEVE FRY

PRAY

Words and Music by
DARLENE ZSCHECH

We call _ up - on _ Your name, _ hum - ble _ our - selves _
We come on bend - ed _ knee, _ we bring _ an of -

_ and _ pray. _ Move in _ our hearts, _ move in _ our
- fer - ing. _ Lead us in Your way _ ev - er - last -

land. _ Ev - 'ry na - tion, tribe,
- ing. _ Ev - 'ry heart of ev -

D.S. al Coda

__ out Your Spir - it, Your won - ders on earth. __ We __ pray, __

CODA

__ out Your Spir - it, Your won - ders on __ earth. __

(Pray, __ pray, __ hum -

- ble our - selves, __ we hum - ble our - selves __ and pray, __

Pour ___ out Your Spir - it, Your won -

- ders on ___ earth. We pray ___ out Your Spir - it, Your won -

- ders on ___ earth. ___

Yeah. ___

READY FOR YOU

Words and Music by
JON MICAH SUMRALL

THE ROBE

Words and Music by WES KING
and PHIL NAISH

An - y - one ___ whose heart is cold and lone - ly,
An - y - one ___ whose feet are tired of walk - ing and
An - y - one ___ who feels that they're un - worth - y,

an - y - one ___ who can't be - lieve, ___ and
e - ven lost ___ their will to run, ___
an - y - one ___ who's just a - fraid, ___

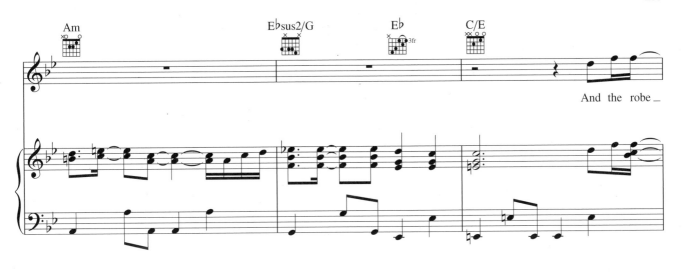

And the robe _

_ is of God that will _ clothe _ your na - ked-

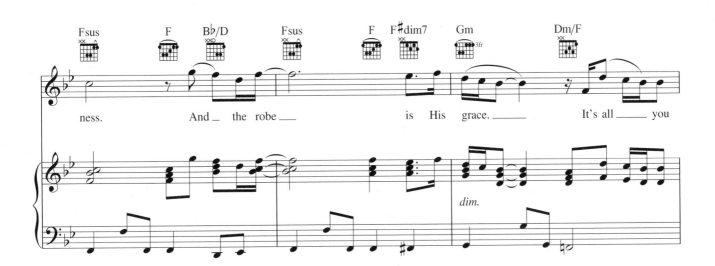

ness. And _ the robe _ is His grace. _ It's all _ you

THIS IS YOUR LIFE

Words and Music by
JONATHAN FOREMAN

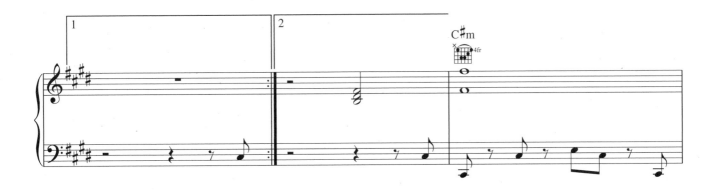

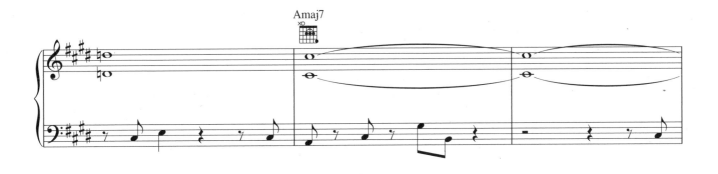

life; is it ev - 'ry - thing _ you dreamed _ that it _ would be _

_ when the world was youn - ger and you had ev - 'ry - thing _ to lose, _

_ you had ev - 'ry - thing _ to lose? _

(Vocal 1st time only)

Repeat and Fade | **Optional Ending**

SONG OF LOVE

Words and Music by REBECCA ST. JAMES,
MATT BRONLEEWE and JEREMY ASH

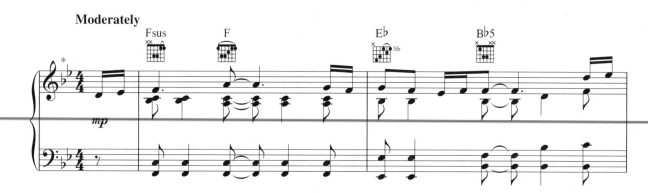

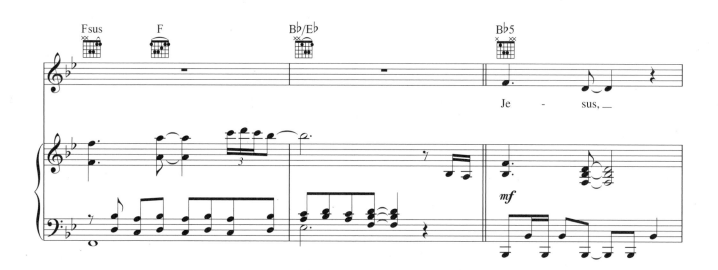

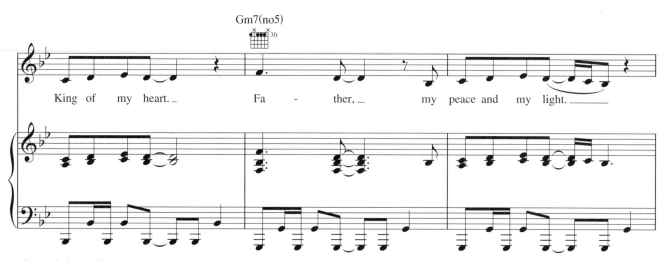

Recorded a half step higher.

SPIRIT THING

Words and Music by PETER FURLER
and STEVE TAYLOR

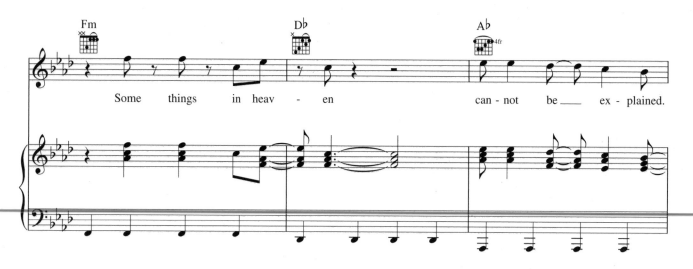

Some things in heav - en can - not be ___ ex - plained.

Yeah, ___ it's just a Spir - it ___ thing, ___ it's just a

ho - ly ___ nudge, it's like a cir - cuit ___ judge ___ in the brain. ___

It's just a Spir - it ___ thing, ___ it's here to

guard my ___ heart, ___ it's just a lit - tle ___ hard ___ to ex - plain. ___

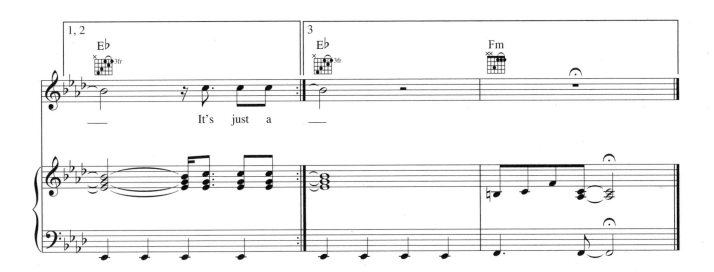

It's just a ___

THESE HANDS

Words and Music by
JEFF DEYO

The sun and moon ___ and ev-'ry ___ star ___ are there to show ___
My ev-'ry move, ___ my ev-'ry ___ breath ___ were meant to point ___
A ten-der thought, ___ a car-ing ___ deed, ___ a gift of love ___

___ me who ___ You are. ___ I can be sure ___ Your fin-ger-prints ___
___ to Your great-ness. ___ There's noth-ing made ___ that was ___ not made ___
___ to one ___ in need. ___ Bring-ing hon-est acts ___ of wor-

THE WAY I WAS MADE

Words and Music by CHRIS TOMLIN,
JESSE REEVES and ED CASH

WELCOME HOME
(You)

Words and Music by BRIAN LITTRELL
and DAN MUCKALA

you to-day. So come and sit down, _____ tell me how you are. __ I know,

son, it's good just to see your face. __

When I

look at ___ you hold-in' my heart, I will give to you all that I

are. _____ I know, son, it's good just to

see your face." __ When I left __ home __ to

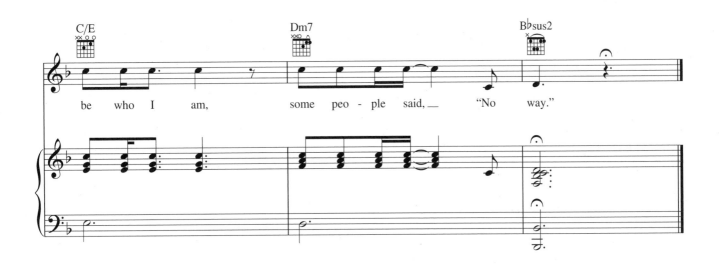

be who I am, some peo-ple said, __ "No way."

WHAT IF HIS PEOPLE PRAYED

Words and Music by MARK HALL
and STEVEN CURTIS CHAPMAN

WHAT MATTERS MOST

Words and Music by
CHERI KEAGGY

* Recorded a half step lower.

WHEN YOU SPOKE MY NAME

Words and Music by BART MILLARD,
NATHAN COCHRAN, MIKE SCHEUCHZER,
JIM BRYSON, ROBBY SHAFFER,
BARRY GRAUL, PETER KIPLEY
and JOEL HANSON

Moderately slow

* Recorded a half step lower.

WHERE THERE IS FAITH

Words and Music by
BILLY SIMON

WISDOM

Words and Music by
TWILA PARIS

I see a mul- ti- tude _ of peo- ple,
There is a mo- ment of __ de- ci- sion,

You are the on - ly way. __ Give us wis - dom. ____

Give us wis - dom. ____

WHOLE AGAIN

Words and Music by
JENNIFER KNAPP

YOU'RE THE VOICE

Words and Music by KEITH REID, ANDY QUANTA,
CHRIS THOMPSON and MAGGIE RYDER

WONDER WHY

Words and Music by GRANT CUNNINGHAM
and MATT HUESMANN